This Anime Sketchbook

 belongs to 

THOMAS ZIMMER
NEUGASSE 23
65520 BAD CAMBERG, GERMANY

Made in the USA
Columbia, SC
21 December 2022

74758880R00074